VICTIM TO VICTORY

A Godly Resource for Empowerment and Hope

Little Sparrow Ministries

Copyright @ 2017 by Little Sparrow Ministries
All Rights Reserved
Printed in the United States of America
International Standard Book Number:
978-1-5323-3761-1

Little Sparrow Ministries
PO Box 307
Lindale, Texas 75771

Email: lsparrowministries@gmail.com

Web site:
littlesparrowministries.com

No part of this book may be reproduced or transmitted in any form or by any means, electronic or mechanical, including photocopying, recording, or by any information storage and retrieval system, without permission in writing from Little Sparrow Ministries.

Scripture quotations marked TLB taken from *The Living Bible*, Copyright @ 2000. Used by permission of Tyndale House Publishers, Inc. Carol Stream, Illinois 60188. All rights reserved.

Scriptures quotations marked NIV taken from *The Holy Bible, New international Version*, Copyright © 1973, 1978, 1984 International Bible Society. Used by permission of Zondervan Bible Publishers.

INGRAM BOOK DISTRIBUTORS

Acknowledgment

I would like to thank everyone who has supported me in writing this book. Tammy Banks has helped me measurably. I ask God to release blessing after blessing on her and her family.

I personally pray for every man or woman who feels trapped in an abusive relationship. I pray they receive direct answers from the Lord as to how to spring the trap door wide open. As a result, they will go into the plans God has for them and their children.

Jeremiah 29:11 NIV

"For I know the plans I have for you," declares the LORD, "plans to prosper you and not to harm you, plans to give you hope and a future."

I also ask you, Lord, to heal and change both parties in these relationships. No doubt there are deep wounds probably from childhood that need to come to the surface so that they can be healed. I decree that every wound would be exposed and come to the light. I also decree that forgiveness would be given. I decree that Godly behaviors will come forth in these relationships. Amen.

Introduction

As you read this book, it is my sincere wish that you will find the direction and hope that you seek at this time.

Many of life's difficulties are never explained satisfactorily to us, but this is the beginning of a time in your life to explore all of the attributes of faith. Without faith, there can't and won't be the future you hope for; but with faith, all things are possible with God.

As you walk this path of emotional and physical pain, there is an answer. Even if you have never thought about God, let alone included Him in your life, He still remains the answer. Just because you do not know Him now does not mean He will not hear your heart's cry. There is nothing you have done or could do that would keep Him from hearing your call for help. He listens intently for that cry just so He can come to your rescue.

In the quietness and loneliness you feel, just call His name. It will mean a turning away from the past and starting a new life with Him. It will mean a life of letting Him be in control. His love is the most awesome thing you can possibly experience. I challenge you today to stop where you are; know that there is a way out, and there is hope for tomorrow!

Hosea 4:6 NIV states, *"My people are destroyed for lack of knowledge."* I am, therefore, going to present to you knowledge, in both the natural (world) and spiritual realm, to help you through this transition in your life.

This book is divided into chapters. The first chapter is information that will help you assess your current situation. If you are abused, you need to start taking action; and you need to ask God for directions for your new life.

The second chapter is spiritual material that will help you in making your transition easier. Remember: Let God be in control. The third chapter is composed of various targeting prayers that will be of help to you. The fourth chapter is composed of targeting prayers for you and your family to pray for the abuser so that God can begin working in his/her life.

The following letter to God might be one that you would at this time write to Him. He will help and direct you. Just ask.

Authors:
Our Lord and Savior, Jesus Christ
Judy H. Farris-Smith

Dear God,

    I can no longer endure this pain. The pain inflicted upon my body is enough, but the emotional and mental strain is more than I can bear.

    Do I bring this despair on myself? How can one person bring out such violence in another? It is humiliating, God, to be controlled with such force and rage.

    I feel so alone God. I find it unbelievable that this has happened, but here I am stripped of everything. I have nowhere to turn, God. Would you help me? Would you show me what I am to do? You are the only hope I have. My life cannot go on this way.

    I really do not even know how to completely trust you. However, from this point on, God, it will be just me and you. Amen.

Your Child

Table of Contents

Chapter One 1
What is Abuse 2
What is Emotional/Verbal Abuse..... 2
What is Physical Abuse.................... 4
Sexual Abuse.................................... 5
Signs They Have not Changed 7
Codependent Behaviors 8
Preparation to Leave 9

Chapter Two 13
Salvation 14
Setting Your Boundaries 17
Generational curses 26
Soul-ties 30
Forgiveness Prayer 33
Spirit of Rejection 34
Word Curses................................... 40
Judgments 43
Speaking Positively 44
I am Victorious............................... 48

Chapter Three 49
   Targeted Prayers for you:
Your Spiritual Authority 50
Believing 51
Blessing.. 53

Boldness 56
Deception 58
Fear 60
Guilt/shame 63
Mental strongholds 65
Peace 67
Protection 69
Trust 72
Joy 74

Chapter Four 75
Targeted Prayers for you and your Family to pray for the abuser:
Salvation 76
Pride 78
Deliverance 80
Generational Curses 82
Bondage 84
Mental Strongholds 86
Holiness 88
Books and References 91
Other Books by LSM 94

CHAPTER ONE

What is Abuse?

What is Emotional Abuse?

What is Physical Abuse?

What is Sexual Abuse

Signs They Have Not Changed

Preparation to Leave

What is Abuse?

"Relationship abuse is a pattern of abusive and coercive behaviors used to maintain power and control over a former or current intimate partner. Abuse can be emotional, financial, sexual or physical and can include threats, isolation, and intimidation. Abuse tends to escalate overtime." *stoprelationshipabuse.org*

The person who is an abuser has mental/emotional problems, is in denial, and will not accept responsibility for their own actions. The only way the person will change is if they will accept responsibility for themselves.

What is Emotional/ Verbal Abuse?

Psychological abuse (also referred to as psychological violence, emotional abuse or mental/verbal abuse) is a form of abuse, characterized by a person subjecting, or exposing, another person to behaviors that may result in psychological trauma, including anxiety, chronic depression, or post-traumatic stress disorder. ***Psychological abuse - Wikipedia***

It can include such behaviors as: threats, insults, constant monitoring, or checking in, excessive texting, humiliation, intimidation, isolation, or stalking. It can also include denying the victim access to money or other basic resources; demeaning the victim in public or in private; undermining the victim's confidence and/or sense of self-worth; convincing the victim that he or she is crazy. Again emotional abuse often escalates into physical violence.

"For women the next most common forms of psychological aggression by an intimate partner are: "insulted, humiliated, made fun of" (58.0%), "acted very angry in a way that seemed dangerous" (57.9%), "told they were a loser, not good enough" (48.9%) and "made threats to physical harm" (45.5%)." **Source:** *National Intimate Partner and Sexual Violence Survey, 2010 Summary Report. National Center for Injury Prevention and Control, Division of Violence Prevention, Atlanta, GA, and Control of the Centers for Disease Control and Prevention.*

For men the next most common forms of psychological aggression by an intimate partner are "called names like fat, ugly, stupid" (51.6%), "told they were a loser, not good enough" (42.4%), "acted very angry in a way that seemed dangerous" (40.4%), and "insulted, humiliated, made fun of" (39.4%)." **Source:** *National Intimate Partner and Sexual Violence Survey, 2010 Summary Report. National Center for Injury Prevention and Control, Division of Violence*

Prevention, Atlanta, GA, and Control of the Centers for Disease Control and Prevention.

What is Physical Abuse?

85% of domestic violence victims are women. **Source:** *Bureau of Justice Statistics Crime Data Brief, Intimate Partner Violence, 1993-2001, February 2003.*

Most cases of domestic violence are never reported to the police. **Source:** *Frieze, I.H., Browne, A. (1989) Violence in Marriage. In L.E. Ohlin & M. H. Tonry, Family Violence. Chicago, IL: University of Chicago Press.*

"Those who have experienced rape, physical violence, and/or stalking by an intimate partner report at least one impact related to experiencing these or other forms of violent behavior in the relationship (e.g., being fearful, concerned for safety, post traumatic stress disorder (PTSD) symptoms, need for health care, injury, contacting a crisis hotline, need for housing services, need for victim's advocate services, need for legal services, missed at least one day of work or school)." **Source:** *National Intimate Partner and Sexual Violence Survey, 2010 Summary Report. National Center for Injury Prevention and Control, Division of Violence Prevention, Atlanta, GA, and Control of the Centers for Disease Control and Prevention.*

Physical abuse can be the following:

1. Hitting, punching, kicking, shoving, choking or slapping you;

2. Using weapons to inflict harm or threaten you;

3. Controlling what you eat or when you sleep;

4. Forcing you to do work against your will;

5. Forcing you to use drugs or alcohol;

6. Stopping you from seeking medical treatment or calling the police.

What is Sexual Abuse?

Sexual abuse is unwanted sexual activity, with perpetrators using force, making threats or taking advantage of victims not able to give consent. Most victims and perpetrators know each other. Immediate reactions to sexual abuse include shock, fear or disbelief. Long-term symptoms include anxiety, fear or post-traumatic stress disorder. While efforts to treat sex offenders remain unpromising, psychological interventions for survivors — especially group therapy — appears effective.

Adapted from the* Encyclopedia of Psychology, *www.apa.org

Approximately 1 in 6 women (16.9%) has experienced sexual violence other than rape by an intimate partner in her lifetime; this includes sexual coercion (9.8%), unwanted sexual contact (6.4%) and non-contact unwanted sexual experiences (7.8%). **Source:** *National Intimate Partner and Sexual Violence Survey, 2010 Summary Report. National Center for Injury Prevention and Control, Division of Violence Prevention, Atlanta, GA, and Control of the Centers for Disease Control and Prevention.*

Nearly one in five women surveyed said they had been raped or had experienced an attempted rape at some point, and one in four reported having been beaten by an intimate partner. One in six women has been stalked, according to the report dated Dec 14, 2011. *www.nytimes.com/2011*

Signs That They Have Not Changed

1. Blames partner or others for his/her behavior.

2. Uses guilt to manipulate the partner into dropping charges or keeping silent.

3. Does not faithfully attend his/her treatment program.

4. Pressures the partner to let him/her move back in before partner is ready.

5. Will not admit he/she was abusive.

6. Convinces others that it is the partner who is either abusive or crazy.

7. Demands to know where partner is and whom he/she is with.

8. Uses partner's behavior as an excuse to treat the partner badly.

9. Continues to use sarcasm or verbal abuse, talk over his/her partner, and shows disrespect or superiority.

10. Does not respond well to complaints or criticism of his/her behavior when he/she slips back into abusive behavior.

11. Continues to undermine partner's authority as a parent, and partner's credibility as a person.

12. Mindset about women/men has not changed, even though he/she avoids being abusive.

13. Criticizes partner for not realizing how much he/she has changed.   ***Escapeabuse.com***

"Completion of a batterer's intervention program class by a man does not mean his victim is safe or that he has stopped being abusive. While men may learn tools for acting nonviolently, research indicates that many men continue to be abusive, even if they change their tactics." ***Embracing Justice: A Resource Guide for Rabbis on Domestic Violence***

At this point, I would inquire of the Lord as to your plans. The spirits of fear and deception will harass and torment you the longer you take to make the decision to leave.

By staying with the abuser, you are surrounding your children with dysfunction.

In the next chapter, there is a section dealing with generational curses. Please read that carefully, and ask the Lord to reveal to you, your generational curses. You will then remove them from yourself and especially your children. Your children need a level playing field to begin their lives.

"Top Ten Questions to Ask About Codependent Behavior

1. Do you avoid confrontation?
2. Do you neglect your needs to attend to another's first?
3. Do you accept verbal or physical abuse by others?
4. Do take responsibility for the actions of others?
5. Do you feel shame when others make mistakes?
6. Do you do more than your share at work, at home or in organizations?
7. Do you ask for help?
8. Do you need others' validation to feel good about yourself?
9. Do you think everyone's feelings are more important than your own?
10. Do you suffer from low self esteem?"

"People with a codependency condition often form or maintain relationships that are one-sided, emotionally destructive and/or abusive verbally or physically." *interventiontreatmentrecovery.org*

"The origins of codependent behavior can be traced back to childhood and family of origin issues. Children in such families learn to avoid feelings and emotions. They learn to define themselves through others' behaviors, successes, or failures. In adulthood, codependents look for approval from others to feel good; they lack self-reflection, a solid concept of self, and the ability to negotiate strong feelings. They seek to save others from poor choices." ***Recoveryconnection.com***

Preparation to Leave

Only you know if and when you are ready to make this transition. You must realize that you are not to blame, and the abuser probably cannot be changed or fixed. Do not hang on to false hopes. The most important question you have to ask yourself is whether or not you are ready to stop this vicious cycle of abuse. If you are, there are certain steps you must take.

If you are physically at risk, do not wait until your plans are made. Seek an attorney or counselor for advice. You may need a restraining order, and an attorney can help you. If you are low on cash, states offer legal aid and many attorneys will provide their services for free.

Also keep a journal on the physical abuse you have encountered. Keep it in a safe place. Keep pictures of bruises or other injuries, or pictures of broken items in your home due to violence. Also keep in a safe place, any medical records verifying that abuse has occurred. I would also include copies of threatening emails, texts etc.

The first thing you will think of is, "Where will I go?" There are safe women's shelters in your area. Those shelters will provide a safe place for you and your children. They should provide you with information regarding legal advice, employment programs, counseling, support groups, and services for your children. You may also have a relative or friend who you could stay with temporarily.

The National Domestic Violence Hotline at 1-800-799-7233 will be able to give you information. Also the web sites, womenslaw.org, www.abanet.org, www.findlaw.com, and teamcares.com/federal_laws.html –Federal Laws and Domestic Violence have valuable information. Advance preparation is recommended. As you take these actions, you will begin to feel more empowered and in control.

1. If you are staying in the area, establish a new mailing address or post office box.

2. Set up a new bank account in your name, along with credit cards, checkbooks, and bank statements. If you have time, save as much cash as you can. I would also take copies of unpaid bills.

3. I would gather my belongings together; everything you want to take with you. If you have children, gather their clothing and toys.

4. Also, gather important papers and documents and make copies of some of them. I would take papers such as birth certificates, passports, Social Security card, health insurance card, driver's license, automobile title, and car

insurance papers. I would also take marriage license, wills, medical records, children's birth certificates, Social Security cards, school records, and immunizations. If you own a home, please take warranty deeds and other valuable information.

5. Remember to take all medications.

6. Make a list of emergency numbers.

Hide everything in bags that cannot be found by the abuser. Also hide an extra set of keys in case the abuser tries to prevent you from leaving. When you are leaving, a call to the police might be in order for extra protection.

I advise you to pray constantly; learn to listen to His voice.

In the next section, are spiritual materials that will help you in this transition.

CHAPTER TWO

Salvation

Setting Boundaries

Generational Curses

Soul-Ties

Forgiveness

Spirit of Rejection

**Word Curses/Judgments/
Speaking Positively**

I am Victorious

Salvation

If you have not asked our Lord into your life, please do so. Pray:

Lord Jesus, forgive my sins. I confess you to be the Christ, the Son of the living God. I receive you as my Lord and Savior. Thank you for washing my sins away with your blood.

Lord Jesus, I thank you for dying on the cross for my sins and for being my Lord and Savior. I ask you to baptize me with your Holy Spirit. I desire to be empowered to be of service and to have the gift of speaking to you in other tongues as the Spirit gives utterance. Thank you Lord. Amen.

Matthew 3:11 NIV *I baptize you with water for repentance. But after me will come one who is more powerful than I, whose sandals I am not fit to carry. He will baptize you with the Holy Spirit and with fire.*

Your abuser's anger and rage more than likely is caused by wrong choices, generational curses, and living in a dysfunctional family in childhood. He/she has not asked the Lord into his/her life and for forgiveness of his/her sins. Therefore, the darkness is within the abuser. There is no light.

Please pray:

Heavenly Father,

I am discouraged because I do not see circumstances changing. I know faith is believing in things that are unseen. Please, Lord, increase my faith.

In the name of Jesus, I bind, break the soul-ties, break your power, and cast out of me: the strongmen of error, anti-Christ, fear, and lying spirits. I shut the open blood line doors that have contributed to me living in darkness. I demand that you separate from me now. Go to the arid places, and never return. Holy Spirit please fill all the void places left by the departing spirits. I loosen right thinking, insights, and revelation.

I know that now you are in control of my life, and the Holy Spirit will guide and direct me. I will put on the garment of praise for the spirit of heaviness. I will rejoice in the Lord, and praise his holy name. Amen.

The Lord has been waiting for you to come to him, listen to him, and read his word. Ask him for directions and truth, before making decisions. Walk closely with him and spend time with him.

He will bring divinely appointed people to you as you need them. He also will open appropriate doors for you to enter at the appointed times in your life. Just ask Him! You need to go to a strong spirit-filled church. Surround yourself with strong Christians. Ask Him, and He will send you a prayer partner.

Matthew 7:7-8 NIV *Ask, and it will be given to you; seek, and you will find; knock and the door will be opened to you. For everyone who asks receives; he who seeks finds, and to him who knocks, the door will be opened.*

James 5:16 NIV *Therefore, confess your sins to each other and pray for each other so that you may be healed. The prayer of a righteous man is powerful and effective.*

Matthew 18:19 NIV *Again, I tell you that if two of you on earth agree about anything you ask for, it will be done for you by my Father in heaven. For where two or three come together in my name, there am I with them.*

SETTING YOUR BOUNDARIES

Because God gave dominion over the earth to man, the only way God can intervene in the life of any one on earth is if they give Him dominion over their life. God gave Adam and Eve boundaries in the Garden of Eden. He told them to eat of every tree except the tree of knowledge of good and evil.

Boundaries are essential to a healthy, balanced life. Boundaries are simply defined as who you are and who you are not. They state your goals and the purposes for your life. Boundaries then safeguard your goals and purposes. They say where you end and another person starts.

They are like property lines. Others can do what they want on their property, but not on yours. Once you set your boundaries, no one gets to redefine these parameters except you and the Lord.

There are many types of boundaries:
personal boundaries,
physical boundaries,
emotional boundaries,
spiritual boundaries,
sexual boundaries.

We must spend time with our Lord. Listen to Him, and ask Him to help you define who you are.

First of all, you must know that you are loved which is essential to all relationships and activities. You must realize that you are a child of God, and that He loves you. He knows every hair on your head. Are you secure in knowing who you are?

Your priorities in life are:

1. God first
2. Yourself
3. Your family
4. What God has called you to do.

When you put yourself as a priority after God, you have started developing correct boundaries.

According to Bill Guiltier, author of **Jesus Set Boundaries**, "Jesus had limitations. He knew he needed nourishment and rest. He also knew he could only be in one place at a time. He had personal needs that took priority in his life. Sometimes those needs took priority over others.

"He did not feel guilty because he knew He had to spend time with God, which gave him focus and energy. So he was never in danger of burn-out, being angry, or depressed.

"Jesus said "no" to inappropriate behaviors of others. He said "no" to control, manipulation, abuse, pride of others, and cynicism. He spoke truth in love to those who were misguided.

"Often he didn't do what people wanted him to do. There were many people he did not help. And whenever he did help other people, he expected them to do their part.

"Guidelines for setting boundaries:

1. Have personal prayer time.
2. Be honest and direct.

Matthew 5:37 NIV *Simply, let your yes be yes, and your no, no; anything beyond this comes from the evil one.*

3. Set priorities.
4. Please God and not people.
5. Obey God."

Boundaries impact all of our lives. We have the responsibility of creating and enforcing our own boundaries.

You must be aware of your limitations. Our physical boundaries must be created so that we know our limitations so we will be safe and appropriate. Physical boundaries refer to our bodies. It is our ability to control when and how others approach us, see us, or touch us.

This boundary separates us from others. It stops with our skin. Some examples are: refusing a hug, locking a door on your bedroom, closing a curtain, building a fence between your home and your neighbor's property.

According to Anne Katherine, author of **Boundaries, Where You End and I Begin**, "Empowerment is the answer. If your physical and sexual boundaries have been violated in the past, you were a victim then, but you do not have to be a victim any longer.

"As of this moment, know that you have the right to determine how your body is treated. Even a light touch can be removed if you do not want it. Simply take his hand off your shoulder and say, "No thank you."

"Move away and say, 'I do not like that.' Or say, 'Please ask permission before you touch me again.' We do not have to be courteous when someone is rude or aggressive. Say, 'Touch me again, and I will scream. I will embarrass you in front of everyone.' When you protect yourself, you empower yourself.

"Our emotional boundaries are our feelings and reactions. We each have our own set of emotional boundaries, and they are individually distinctive." They will help us disengage with manipulative and controlling emotions of others.

We respond to the world based on our values, beliefs, goals, and concerns. When your emotional boundaries are well-developed, you are in charge of your own feelings, moods, and problems.

You can be compassionate toward others without taking on their feelings or problems and making them your own. Our emotional health is related to the health of our boundaries.

Another sign of emotional boundaries is learning to take responsibility for ourselves. This may mean at times we must confront inappropriate behavior. We may have to back off helping someone and direct them to someone else.

Boundaries can be spoken or unspoken. Walking away from a person who is insulting you, speaks as loudly as your words. I set limits on what people say about me. When you let someone verbally abuse you or hurt you, you have not protected your personal boundaries. Do not let them cross the line. Setting a boundary means you respect yourself. When you respect yourself, you protect yourself from inappropriate behavior.

Spiritual boundaries help us to distinguish God's will from our own.

Matthew 6:33 NIV *But seek first his kingdom and his righteousness, and all these things will be given to you.*

Through God, we will find peace, contentment, and right thinking. We instinctively will know who we can talk to about our spiritual beliefs and who we cannot.

Mental/Intellectual boundaries give us the freedom to have our own thoughts and opinions. Sexual boundaries are the choices we make as to who we interact with sexually and to what extent. You know what is safe and appropriate.

Remember the purpose of setting boundaries is to **take care of you**, not to create walls. Say no to obligations that make you miserable. Protect your health. By saying, "no" to more things, you will then have the time, energy and resources to get really good at the things you want to say "yes" to.

Boundaries should be clear, specific, reasonable, and enforceable. An example is telling your son that you will buy him a car, but he has to pay for his own car insurance, maintenance, and fuel.

I want to tell you a personal example. I was with a group of ministry people, and we were to visit a very large ministry in downtown Washington, DC. They were in the middle of a large project that was extremely time-consuming. The individual who was showing us around the organization started demanding that we all help them.

She confronted each one of us individually. The other people in my group said that they would do something. I said "no", and that was it. When we got back to our van, some of the people said, "Judy, you had the courage to say 'no'." They had wished they had done so.

Another example, my son and I were going to visit my family that we had not seen for several years. I want to let you know that my mother had a serious control problem.

We arrived at our destination by plane and were taken to my sister's home to refresh ourselves. We then decided that we would go to see our mother.

Upon arriving at her home, I went up to the door. She started to yell at me for not getting there sooner. She had not seen her grandson in four years, and all she did was get us upset.

So, I said to everyone, "Get back in the car, we are leaving here." I believe that was my first experience in really setting my boundaries. I was proud of myself, and I knew from then on I was going to have healthy boundaries.

With good boundaries, we can have the wonderful assurance that comes from knowing we can and will protect ourselves from the ignorance, meanness, or thoughtlessness of others.

According to Anne Katherine, "We learn about our boundaries by the way we are treated as children. Then we teach others where our boundaries are by the way we let them treat us."

"Most people will respect our boundaries, if we indicate where they are. With some people, however, we must actively defend them. In healthy relationships, people respect each other's boundaries. Each person respects the needs, values, thoughts, and feelings of the other, regardless how they differ from their own.

"When respect is reciprocal, the self-worth of both people will probably increase. Without boundaries, you will limit God's plan for you. You must set limits in order to live the life God has planned for you." I do recommend that you read the book by Anne Katherine, ***Where You End and I Begin***.

Prayer for Establishing Healthy Boundaries

Heavenly Father,

I repent for not setting up healthy boundaries. Growing up I was surrounded by dysfunctional people who constantly crossed my boundary lines. As you know, I did not have healthy relationships.

Lord, please help me with establishing healthy boundaries which include physical, emotional, personal, spiritual, and sexual boundaries. I surrender this dysfunctional area of my life to you. I ask for your wisdom, revelation, and insights. Also, Lord, I need boldness and courage.

Thank you, Lord, for molding and remaking me in your image. Amen.

Another area that needs to be dealt with is Generational Curses. What we are doing is trying to prevent barriers between you and God so that you can hear clearly.

Lamentations 5:7 NIV *Our fathers sinned and are no more, and we bear their punishment.*

Prayers for Breaking Generational Curses

Ask the Holy Spirit to show you what curses have been placed on you and your ancestors. You need to break curses allowed by: God, Satan who has a legal right, and Satan who does not have a legal right. Please pray the following prayers out loud in the order indicated:

Prayer for Breaking Curses Allowed by God

Heavenly Father,

Heavenly Father, I come to you in the name of our Lord Jesus Christ and by virtue of his shed blood, I ask you to forgive me of my sins and the sins of my forefathers, those that are known and are not known. Lord, I ask that you remove and completely destroy all the roots and seeds of my own personal sins and my ancestors' sins.

I ask you to separate me (and my children) from the generational curse or curses that you have allowed on my life as a result of the sins of my forefathers or my own personal sins. I now shut the blood line doors that were opened as a result of my sins and my ancestors' sins. Thank you, Lord. Amen.

Prayer for Breaking Curses From Satan Having Legal Authority

The book by Dr. Carol Robeson, *Strongman's His Name...What's His Game?*, teaches about the sixteen biblically-based strongmen that may have gained strongholds over different areas of your life.

Heavenly Father,

I repent for my sins and my ancestors' sins that are known and unknown. I know that you have forgiven me.

By the authority and power given to me by the holy name of our Lord, Jesus Christ, I bind, break the soul-ties, break your power, and cast off of me the strongmen of:

spirit of divination,

familiar spirit,
spirit of jealousy,
lying spirit,
perverse spirit,
spirit of haughtiness,
spirit of heaviness,
spirit of whoredoms,
spirit of infirmity,
dumb and deaf spirit,
spirit of bondage,
spirit of fear,
seducing spirits,
spirit of anti-Christ,
spirit of error,
spirit of death

and all other demonic spirits that were associated with any and all generational curses which include familiar spirits, familial spirits, and dormant spirits. I now shut the blood line doors that were opened as a result of my sins and my ancestors' sins. I demand that you separate from me now as you have no legal right to stay. Go to the arid places, and never return. Holy Spirit please come and fill the void places within me. Amen.

Prayer for Breaking Curses from Satan and Demonic Spirits that Do Not Have a Legal Right

Before doing this prayer, you will need to do some research into your family line. Find the negative occurrences (generational curses) in your family line. A few examples are torment, codependence, divorce, abortion, poverty, abuse, anger, offense, rejection, mental problems, negative thoughts, cancer, and arthritis. Make a list.

In the next prayer, you will use your authority given to you by our Lord, Jesus Christ. Please insert the names of any demonic spirits that have tormented and harassed you and your ancestors. Take them from your list.

Heavenly Father,

By the authority and power given to me by the holy name of our Lord, Jesus Christ, I demand these curses of _____ (e.g. poverty, cancer, abuse, codependence, anger) to be broken now and forever more. I bind, break the soul-ties, break your power, and cast out of me all strongmen and all demonic spirits, familiar spirits, familial spirits, and dormant spirits that were associated with these curses.

I demand you to separate from me now as you have no legal right to stay. I shut the blood line doors that were open and caused these curses in my life. Go to the arid places, and never return. Holy Spirit please come and fill the void places within me. Amen.

Ungodly Soul-Ties

A soul-tie can be described as the linking together of two individuals, i.e. becoming one in their souls. God designed a soul-tie as a two-way interaction for the flow of love between two parties. Godly soul-ties are created between friends and family members.

According to the authors, Bill and Sue Banks, ***Breaking Unhealthy Soul-Ties,*** "Ungodly soul-ties are created between individuals as a result of sins. If relationships are based on dependence, bondage or idolatry, an unhealthy soul-tie has developed. Also, relationships can become ungodly as a result of adultery, manipulation, control, or co-dependency. An ungodly soul-tie can develop between you and a substance that develops into an addiction."

If possible, please destroy all pictures or personal items belonging to anyone with whom you have an ungodly soul-tie.

Prayer to Break Ungodly Soul-Ties

Heavenly Father,

In the name of Jesus, I break the ungodly soul-tie with _____ (name).

I ask that you cleanse me from all unrighteousness as a result of any known or unknown agreement that resulted in an ungodly soul-tie. I ask that you sever all strongholds that have formed as a result of this ungodly action. Forgive me, Lord, for my part in creating this ungodly soul-tie.

I also ask you to heal my emotions and to assemble and heal all the fragmented pieces of my soul. I decree that my soul has been restored. I plead the blood of Christ over my spirit, soul, and body. Amen.

Prayer to Break Godly Soul-ties

To break the soul-tie with the deceased, divorced, or abandoned spouse, parent, or friend, pray the following prayer:

Heavenly Father,

In the name of Jesus, I break the soul-tie with _____ (name).

I ask you, Lord, to heal my emotions, to assemble, and to heal all the fragmented pieces of my soul. I decree that my soul has been restored. I plead the blood of Christ over my spirit, soul, and body. Lord, I ask that you transfuse my blood line with yours; thereby, eliminating anything unholy to a blood line of purity and holiness. Amen.

There may be situations where family members are heavily involved in the occult or other sins. These sins could be affecting you or your family adversely. If this is the case, sever the soul-tie. Children may need to break soul-ties in order for them to move on with their lives.

Forgiveness Prayer

Heavenly Father,

Forgive me for harboring any unforgiveness, resentment, and bitterness. Please reveal to my mind those that I have offended or need to forgive.

Help me, Holy Spirit, to stay obedient to our Lord, and convict me of all my wrong doings so that I may walk closer to the light. Amen.

Please pray the following for those who you have offended or you need to forgive.

Lord, forgive me for whatever I have done to _____ (name of person).

Lord, forgive _____ (name of person) for whatever they have done to me.

Lord, I forgive _____ (name of person).

Lord, forgive us for what we have both done to you.

I release _____ (name of person).

Spirit of Rejection

Rejection is an act of denying love to someone. When we are rejected by others, we can also reject ourselves.

Rejection is a spirit. I believe that there are several other spirits that work closely with rejection to bring dysfunction into our lives and our families. Some of these are the strongman of lying spirits, and the spirits of deception, and heaviness.

How can it come into our lives? It can create bondages in our lives due to generational curses. These evil spirits may have entered your family blood line many years ago. It could have happened as a result of someone denying family members love and affection. It could be a result of marrying dysfunctional people. It could be a result of alcoholism, divorce, abandonment, or a controlling relationship.

Some of the characteristics of a person having a spirit of rejection are the following:

Sarcasm and ridicule
Compulsively clean
Perfectionism
Anger and rage

Eating disorder/self-mutilation
Depression
Suicide

Inwardly a person feeling rejected demonstrates shame, disgrace, embarrassment, regret, dishonor, humiliation, and condemnation. They feel that they are not wanted, not loved, not appreciated, and not good enough. A person performs or strives to earn their acceptance. They believe that they are loved for what they do rather that for who they are.

The lying spirits continually reinforce their dysfunctional beliefs with spirits of deception, accusations, slander, gossip, and lies. The spirit of heaviness brings in sorrow, self-pity, despair, hopelessness, broken hearted, depression, and suicidal tendencies.

Our spirit is the Holy Spirit within us. It is meant to influence our minds and emotions. The person with the spirit of rejection allows Satan and his evil spirits to control our minds and emotions. The enemy is continually at work to divide us from God, and to create disunity in our families.

God loves us and wants to take away our pain. But first, He wants us to have an understanding of how the enemy operates. There are evil spirits that can harass us and torment us on a daily basis. Their sole function is to kill, steal, and destroy God's people.

We must fight continually against the weapons of the enemy. We are all in continual warfare. We are not alone. Get a prayer partner, and pray together on a daily basis. There is power in agreement. We must target our prayers. Pray specific not general prayers. Learn the enemies' names, and demand them to leave.

Let us first deal with the person who has caused you to feel rejected. You must forgive that person. The Lord knows how much that person has wounded you, but you must forgive.

Matthew 6:14-15 NIV *For if you forgive men when they sin against you, your heavenly Father will also forgive you. But if you do not forgive men their sins, your Father will not forgive your sins.*

If you need to, please pray the Forgiveness Prayer again.

Prayers for Rejection Issues

Prayer of Repentance for the Spirit of Self-Rejection

Heavenly Father,

I repent for rejecting myself. I repent for all the negative things I have thought and said about myself. I repent of not accepting myself, and for trying to be someone I was never meant to be. I repent for not believing that I have worth and value, just as I am.

I turn away from rejecting myself, and I renounce all the lies I have believed about myself. I renounce and break every curse I have thought or spoken about myself. I choose to accept myself. I break all soul-ties with self-rejection, heaviness, deception, lying spirits, and every spirit that would lead me to reject myself.

Lord, I ask you to separate me from all generational curses and vows that have caused this spirit of rejection and other spirits associated with it to have an open door in my life. I demand that all the roots of rejection are destroyed, and that all the blood line doors that have caused rejection are closed.

I cast the spirit of rejection off of me, and I ask the Holy Spirit to fill me with his truth. Holy Spirit, please come and fill all the void places within me. Amen.

Prayer of Repentance for the Fear of Rejection

Heavenly Father,

I repent for allowing the fear of rejection in my life. I repent of all lying, deception, suspicion, mistrust, control, or manipulation that I have allowed to operate in my mind and behavior.

Lord, I repent of trying to please people instead of you. I repent of my self-protective behavior and all self-pity. And now, I renounce the fear of rejection and all my destructive behaviors.

I renounce and break all soul-ties and generational ties to the fear of rejection, and I break its hold on my life. I refuse to be bound to this fear any longer, and I ask you to help me break down this wall of fear of rejection. I decree that this wall of rejection is broken. Amen.

Prayer for Repentance for Rejecting God

Heavenly Father,

I am sorry for all the times and all the ways I have rejected you. Please forgive me. I repent for not believing you, for not listening to you, and for refusing your love. I repent for not trusting you, and for doubting your love for me. I repent for all the stubbornness, pride, self-will, and rebellion that I have walked in.

In the name of Jesus, I renounce all rejection of God. I renounce all involvement with any spirit that would lead me to reject God.

I renounce and break all vows and covenants, all soul-ties and generational ties that would bind me to the rejection of God.

I choose to love God with all my heart, with all my soul, and with my entire mind. Amen.

Parts of some of these prayers are found in Chris Hayward's book, ***The End of Rejection.***

Word Curses, Judgments, and Speaking Positively

1 Peter 3:10 NIV For, whoever would love life and see good days must keep his tongue from evil and his lips from deceitful speech.

Matthew 12:34-37 NIV ...for out of the overflow of the heart the mouth speaks. The good man brings good things out of the good stored up in him, and the evil man brings evil things out of the evil stored up in him. But I tell you that men will have to give account on the Day of Judgment for every careless word they have spoken. For by your words you will be acquitted, and by your words you will be condemned.

James 3:9-10 NIV With the tongue we praise our Lord and Father and with it we curse men, who have been made in God's likeness. Out of the same mouth come praise and cursing. My brothers, this should not be.

Psalm 52:2-4 NIV Your tongue plots destruction; it is like a sharpened razor, you who practice deceit. You love evil rather than good and falsehood rather than speaking the truth. You love every harmful word, O you deceitful tongue!

Proverbs 12:18 NIV   *Reckless words pierce like a sword, but the tongue of the wise brings healing.*

Proverbs 10:18-21 NIV   *He who conceals his hatred has lying lips, and whoever spreads slander is a fool. When words are many, sin is not absent, but he who holds his tongue is wise. The tongue of the righteous is choice silver, but the heart of the wicked is of little value. The lips of the righteous nourish many, but fools die for lack of judgment.*

1 Corinthians 4:12-13 NIV   *…When we are cursed, we bless; when we are persecuted, we endure it; when we are slandered, we answer kindly.*

Deuteronomy 30:7 NIV   *The Lord your God will put all these curses on your enemies who hate and persecute you.*

Luke 6:28 NIV   *Bless those who curse you, pray for those who mistreat you.*

Word Curses

Negative words are harmful. Casual and/or destructive remarks often become self-fulfilling prophecies.

We can easily internalize destructive words. This internalization can govern our future behavior because our behavior or actions usually follow spoken words. As a result, Satan has gained a foothold in our lives by establishing a seedbed of lies.

Wrongful prayers, gossip, and slander are examples of word curses. Prayers that try to control and manipulate someone according to another's fleshly desires are an abomination to God.

The sin of murder is committed when one gossips or slanders another. They not only can kill a person's reputation but also can physically harm them.

Note: In order to see the hand of God work in our lives, we must forgive those who have harmed us. Do not let a root of bitterness develop.

Judgments

Judge: to make up one's mind about; form an opinion or estimate about; to think; suppose; conclude; to criticize; blame; and condemn. Judgment: a decision; decree; a decision made by anybody who judges; a misfortune thought of as a punishment from God. (***The World Book Dictionary 1981 Edition.***)

Romans 14:10 NIV   *You, then, why do you judge your brother? Or why do you look down on your brother? For we all stand before God's judgment seat.*

James 2:*13* NIV   *…because judgment without mercy will be shown to anyone who has not been merciful. Mercy triumphs over judgment.*

Luke 6:37 NIV   *Do not judge, and you will not be judged. Do not condemn, and you will not be condemned. Forgive, and you will be forgiven.*

Speaking Positively

If we carefully scrutinize our vocabulary, we can determine where we are spiritually. Are we bringing God's truth into the world by speaking positively or are we bringing in the enemy's darkness by speaking negatively?

Our behaviors or actions usually follow our spoken words, and our spoken words reveal the true condition of our hearts. As we speak positive and edifying words, we confirm the word of God in our lives and in others.

Psalm 12:6 NIV   *And the words of the Lord are flawless, like silver, refined in a furnace of clay, purified seven times.*

Psalm 33:6 NIV   *By the word of the Lord were the heavens made; their starry host by the breath of his mouth.*

Matthew 8:8 NIV   *The centurion replied, "Lord, I do not deserve to have you come under my roof. But just say the word, and my servant will be healed." (The centurion had faith in the power of the spoken word of Jesus.)*

Matthew 17:20 NIV *He replied, "Because you have so little faith, I tell you the truth, if you have faith as small as a mustard seed, you can say to this mountain, 'Move from here to there' and it will move. Nothing will be impossible for you."* (He said just speak to those things that are not as though they were.)

Mark 11:23 NIV *I tell you the truth, if anyone says to this mountain, "Go throw yourself into the sea," and does not doubt in his heart but believes that what he says will happen, it will be done for him.*

John 15:7-8 NIV *If you remain in me and my words remain in you, ask whatever you wish, and it will be given you. This is to my Father's glory, that you bear much fruit, showing yourselves to be my disciples.*

Prayer for Breaking Word Curses/ Judgments

Heavenly Father,

By the authority and power given to me by the holy name of our Lord, Jesus Christ, I demand all word curses, judgments, assignments, and all curses from witchcraft, jealousy, envy, and strife are broken and shattered.

I demand that all strongmen and demonic spirits that are associated with these curses to separate from me now. Go to the arid places, and never return. In the name of Jesus, I ask you to send blessings and conviction to the originator. Holy Spirit, I ask you to come and fill all the void places within me.

I decree that all word curses, judgments, and schemes and plans of the enemy are broken and shattered. Amen.

I personally use the above prayer on a regular basis. I stay away from gossiping people, and try to scrutinize my words daily. Curses can harm us physically, spiritually, and emotionally.

Prayer for Speaking Positively

Heavenly Father,

In the name of Jesus, I ask for ears to hear, eyes to see, and a mouth that speaks spiritual truths. I ask that your truths penetrate my innermost being so my words are always positive and edifying. I ask for a new mind-set so that my thoughts, attitudes, and actions are always positive even in the middle of difficult or dark circumstances.

I prophetically decree that from this day forth I will speak blessings over myself and others, and that I will speak to those things that are not as though they were. Please help me, Lord, by opening my natural eyes to see the impact my positive and edifying words have over my life and the lives of others.

Lord, I ask that you take me to a new level of faith and spiritual maturity. Amen.

I am Victorious

I am God's child, born again of the incorruptible seed. (1 Peter 1:23)

I am set free. (John 8:31-33)

I am protected by the power of his name. (John 17:11)

I am kept from the evil one. (John 17:15)

I am dead to sin and alive to God in Christ Jesus. (Romans 6:11)

I am free from the power of sin. (Romans 6:14)

I am more than a conqueror through Christ. (Romans 8:37)

I am the strongest when I am weakest. (2 Corinthians 12:9)

I am chosen by God to be holy and blameless. (Ephesians 1:4)

I am becoming mature, the measure of the stature of the fullness of Christ. (Ephesians 4:13)

I have been delivered from the domain of darkness and transferred to the kingdom of God. (Colossians 1:13)

I am filled with God's power that works mightily in me. (Colossians 1:29)

I am Victorious. (Revelation 21:7)

HALLELUJAH, HALLELUJAH, HALLELUJAH!

CHAPTER THREE

Targeted Prayers for you:

Your Spiritual Authority

Believing

Blessings

Boldness

Deception

Fear

Guilt/Shame

Mental Strongholds

Peace

Protection

Trust

Your Spiritual Authority

Luke: 10:19 NIV   ...*I have given you authority to trample on snakes and scorpions (demons and evil spirits) and to overcome all the power of the enemy; nothing will harm you.*

Matthew 28:18 NIV   *All authority in heaven and earth has been given to me. God himself is the power behind our authority.* (The devil and his forces are obliged to recognize our authority.)

God has given us the power and authority to drive out evil spirits and to restore our soul, mind, and body. The **tongue** is the weapon to be used to demonstrate this power and authority. The enemy cannot hear our thoughts. Praying a prayer in silence renders it ineffective. We must verbally address the enemy. The **prayer of agreement** is another weapon to be used with the **tongue**. When praying, use God's scriptures and personalize them. Declare and decree that what you are praying for has already been accomplished.

Kenneth Hagin states in his book, ***The Believer's Authority***, *"All the authority that can be exercised upon the earth has to be exercised through the Church, because Christ is not here in person – in his physical body."* Use your authority! (Church: body of Christ)

Believing

Lord this is your word and your word is truth:

Luke 8:11-12 NIV   *This is the meaning of the parable: The seed is the word of God. Those along the path are the ones who hear, and then the devil comes and takes away the word from their hearts, so that they may not believe and be saved.*

2 Corinthians 5:7 NIV *We live by faith not by sight.*

Romans 15:13 NIV   *May the God of hope fill you with all joy and peace as you trust in him, so that you may overflow with hope by the power of the Holy Spirit.*

John 20:31 NIV   *But these are written so you may believe that Jesus is the Christ, the Son of God, and that by believing you may have life in his name.*

Targeted Prayer:

Heavenly Father,

In the name of Jesus, I bind, break the soul-ties, break your power, and cast off of me, the strongmen of lying spirits, bondage, anti-Christ, error, familiar spirit, all dormant spirits, and familial spirits. I demand you to separate from me now as you have no legal right to stay. I shut all the blood lines doors that have contributed to my unbelief. I demand you to go to the arid places, and never return. You cannot attach yourself to me or anyone else. Holy Spirit please come and fill the void places within me.

I am asking you to increase my faith. You will judge the person who has been troubling and confusing me. (Galatians 5:10 TLB) For it is by believing in my heart that I am made right with you, and it is by confessing with my mouth that I am saved. (Romans 10:10 TLB) Abraham never wavered in believing God's promises. In fact, his faith grew stronger. In this, he brought glory to God. (Romans 4:20 TLB) I decree that from this day forward, I will not waver in believing your promises. Amen

Note: Matthew 18:18 NIV, it states, *"...whatsoever ye shall bind on earth shall be bound in heaven and whatsoever ye shall loose on earth shall be loosed in heaven."*

We bind the demonic and loose the opposite or positive in a person's life. We cannot demand or cast it out of a person if they are an unwilling participant. Binding and loosing is a strong spiritual weapon to be used.

Blessings

Lord this is your word and your word is truth:

Proverbs 13:21 TLB   *Trouble chases sinners, while blessings chase the righteous.*

Proverbs 10:6 TLB   *The godly are showered with blessings; evil people cover up their harmful intentions.*

Psalms 119:58 TLB   *With all my heart, I want your blessings. Be merciful just as you promised.*

Psalms 85:12 TLB   *Yes, the Lord pours down his blessings. Our land will yield its bountiful crops.*

Psalms 31:19 TLB   *Oh, how great is your goodness to those who publicly declare that you will rescue them. For you have stored up great blessings for those who trust and reverence you.*

Ephesians 3:6 TLB   *And this is the secret plan: The Gentiles have an equal share with the Jews in all the riches inherited by God's children. Both groups have believed the Good News, and both are part of the same body and enjoy together the promise of blessings through Christ Jesus.*

1 Corinthians 9:23 TLB *I do all this to spread the Good News, and in doing so I enjoy its blessings.*

Zechariah 8:12 TLB *For I am planting seeds of peace and prosperity among you. The grapevines will be heavy with fruit. The earth will produce its crops, and the sky will release the dew. Once more I will make the remnant in Judah and Israel the heirs of these blessings.*

Isaiah 29:23 TLB *For when they see their many children and material blessings, they will recognize the holiness of the Holy One of Israel. They will stand in awe of the God of Israel.*

Targeted Prayer:

Heavenly Father,

In the name of Jesus, I bind all evil communication, plans, and schemes that would prevent me from receiving victory over evil and from receiving the Lord's blessings that he has intended for me. I loosen all the rich blessings he has intended for me, one gracious blessing after another. (John 1:16 TLB)

Your word says, *"That you will cause your people and their homes around your holy hill to be a blessing. And you will send showers, showers of blessings, which will come just when they are needed."* (Ezekiel 34:26 TLB)

Isaiah 44:3 TLB *For I will give you abundant water to quench your thirst and to moisten your parched fields. And I will pour out my Spirit and my blessings on your children.*

I thank you, Lord, for your word, because your word does not come back void. I prophetically decree that your blessings are chasing the righteous (me) before the watching world. Amen.

Repeat the scriptures to the Lord and remind him that his words do not come back void.

Boldness

Lord this is your word and your word is truth:

Luke 11:8 NIV   *I tell you, though he will not get up and give him the bread because he is his friend, yet because of the man's boldness he will get up and give him as much as he needs.*

Acts 4:29 NIV   *Now, Lord, consider their threats and enable your servants to speak your word with great boldness.*

Proverbs 28:1 NIV   *The wicked man flees though no one pursues, but the righteous are as bold as a lion.*

2 Timothy 1:7 NIV   *For God did not give us a spirit of timidity, but a spirit of power, of love, and self-discipline.*

Psalms 138:3 NIV   *When I called, you answered me; you made me bold and stouthearted.*

Targeted Prayer:

Heavenly Father,

In the power and authority of our Lord and Savior, Jesus Christ, I bind, break the soul-ties, break your power, and cast out of me the strongmen of fear. Separate from me now as you have no legal right to stay. I demand you to go the arid places, and never return. Holy Spirit please fill every void place within me.

Lord, give me the boldness of David confronting Goliath, and give me the power and boldness demonstrated by other men and women in your word. Speak through my mouth, and use this vessel to your glory. Holy Spirit, please guide and direct me. I am here, Lord; use me. I decree that I have boldness, and I am being used by my God. Amen.

Deception

Lord this is your word and your word is truth:

Psalms 12:2 NIV   *Everyone lies to his neighbor; their flattering lips speak with deception.*

Proverbs 26:26 NIV   *His malice may be concealed by deception, but his wickedness will be exposed in the assembly.*

Jeremiah 9:6 NIV   *You live in the midst of deception; in their deceit they refuse to acknowledge me, declares the Lord.*

Proverbs 14:8 NIV   *The wisdom of the prudent is to give thought to their ways, but the folly of fools is deception.*

2 Corinthians 4:2 NIV   *Rather, we have renounced secret and shameful ways; we do not use deception, nor do we distort the word of God. On the contrary, by setting forth the truth plainly we commend ourselves to every man's conscience in the sight of God.*

Targeted Prayer

Heavenly Father,

We live in a world controlled by the evil one, but thankfully, we are not of this world. For the ungodly, deception has become a way of life, and they refuse to acknowledge you, Lord.

As your children, we live by your word. John 8:31-32 NIV states, *"If you hold to my teaching, you are really my disciples. Then you will know the truth, and the truth will set you free."*

In the name of Jesus, I bind, break the soul-ties, break your power, and cast out of me the strongman of lying spirits and the spirit of deception. I shut all blood line doors that were opened due to deception. I demand that you separate from me now. Go to the arid places, and never return. Holy Spirit please fill all void places within me.

Lord, I ask you to loosen truth and discernment. As darkness and deception surround me, I now have the ability to see the truth, and will not be caught in the web of the enemy's lies. I decree that I will no longer walk in deception. Amen.

Fear /Anxiety/Worry

Lord, this is your word and your word is truth:

Romans 8:15 NIV *For you did not receive a spirit of slavery to fall back into fear, but you received the spirit of adoption, by whom we cry out, "Abba, Father!"*

Hebrews 13:6 NIV *So we say with confidence, the Lord is my helper, and I will not be afraid. What can man do to me?*

1 John 4:18 NIV *There is no fear in love. But perfect love drives out fear, because fear has to do with punishment. The one who fears is not made perfect in love.*

Proverbs 3:25-26 NIV *Have no fear of sudden disaster or of the ruin that overtakes the wicked, for the Lord will be your confidence and will keep your foot from being snared.*

Psalms 23:4 NIV *Even though I walk through the valley of the shadow of death, I will fear no evil, for you are with me; your rod and your staff they comfort me.*

Psalms 27:1-3 NIV *The Lord is my light and my salvation - whom shall I fear? The Lord is the stronghold of my life - of whom shall I be afraid? When evil men advance against me to devour my flesh, when my enemies and my foes attack me, they will stumble and fall.*

Psalms 56:11 NIV   *In God I trust; I will not be afraid. What can man do to me?*

Isaiah 41:13 NIV   *For I am the Lord, your God, who takes hold of your right hand and says to you, "Do not fear; I will help you."*

John 14:27 NIV   *Peace I leave with you, my peace I give you; I do not give to you as the world gives. Do not let your hearts be troubled and do not be afraid.*

2 Timothy 1:7 TLB   *For God has not given us a spirit of fear and timidity, but of power, love, and self-discipline.*

God's love will remove all fear. However, we must make a decision not to entertain fearful thoughts. We must **TRUST** God in all things.

Targeted Prayer: *(Whenever the strongman of fear tries to surface, repeat the following prayer.)*

Heavenly Father,

In the name of Jesus, I bind, break the soul-ties, break your power, and cast out of me the strongmen of fear and lying spirits, as well as the spirits of anxiety and confusion. I demand you to separate from me now. I shut all blood line doors that were opened due to the spirit of fear. You have no legal right to stay. Go to the arid places, and never return. Do not attach yourself to anyone or anything.

Holy Spirit, I ask that you fill every void place left by the departing spirits. Fill me with your peace. Please take my mind captive so that it is filled with trust, faith, and belief.

I surrender the situation of _____ to you. I no longer will carry this burden because it is now on your shoulders. I decree that I trust my God, and I will no longer carry the burden of fear, worry, or anxiety. Amen.

Guilt/Shame

Lord, this is your word, and your word is truth:

Psalms 32:1 NIV   *Blessed is he whose transgressions are forgiven, whose sins are covered.*

Psalms 32:5 NIV   *Then I acknowledged my sin to you and did not cover up my iniquity. I said, "I will confess my transgressions to the Lord" and you forgave the guilt of my sins. "Selah."*

Psalms 39:8 NIV   *Save me from all my transgressions; do not make me the scorn of fools.*

Psalms 65:3 NIV   *When we were overwhelmed by sins, you forgave our transgressions.*

Psalms 103:12 NIV   *As far as the east is from the west, so far has he removed our transgressions from us.*

Isaiah 43:25 NIV   *I, even I, am he who blots out your transgressions, for my own sake, and remembers your sins no more.*

1 John 1:9 NIV   *If we confess our sins, he is faithful and just and will forgive us our sins and purify us from all unrighteousness.*

Romans 9:33 NIV *As it is written: "See, I lay in Zion a stone that causes men to stumble and a rock that makes them fall, and the one who trusts in him will never be put to shame."*

Targeted Prayer:

Heavenly Father,

In the name of Jesus, I bind, break the soul-ties, break your power, and cast out of me the strongmen of lying spirits and bondage. I demand you to separate from me now. Go to the arid places, and never return. Do not attach yourselves to anyone or anything. Holy Spirit fill every void place left by the departing spirits.

Through the grace and mercy of Jesus Christ, I am saved. My sins are not remembered. He has blotted out my transgression, and I am forgiven. If Jesus can forgive me, then I must forgive myself. I decree that I will no longer listen to the lies of the enemy. I have been purified from all unrighteousness; I trust in him, and I will never be put to shame. I am a child of the Most High. Thank you, Lord. Amen.

Mental Strongholds

Lord this is your word and your word is truth:

Romans 12:2 NIV *Do not conform any longer to the pattern of this world, but be transformed by the renewing of your mind. Then you will be able to test and approve what God's will is - his good, pleasing, and perfect will.*

2 Corinthians 10:4-5 NIV *The weapons we fight with are not the weapons of the world. On the contrary, they have divine power to demolish strongholds. We demolish arguments and every pretension that sets itself up against the knowledge of God, and we take captive every thought to make it obedient to Christ.*

Romans 8:6 NIV *The mind of the sinful man is death, but the mind controlled by the Spirit is life and peace.*

Isaiah 26:3 NIV *You will keep in perfect peace him whose mind is steadfast, because he trusts in you.*

2 Timothy 1:7 NIV *For God did not give us a spirit of timidity, but a spirit of power, of love and self-discipline.*

Targeted Prayer:

Heavenly Father,

I am having trouble keeping my mind in perfect peace. The enemy is creating mine fields in my mind, and as a result confusion reigns. If there are strongholds in my life that need to be destroyed, guide and direct me so that I can shut these open doors. If there is a forgiveness problem, convict me.

In the name of Jesus, I bind, break the soul-ties, break your power, and cast out of me the strongmen of dumb and deaf spirits, lying spirits, fear, and heaviness, as well as the spirits of mental illness, insanity, suicide, crying, familial spirits, and confusion. I demand that you separate from me now. I shut the open blood line doors that are allowing mental strongholds. Go to the arid places, and never return. Holy Spirit please fill all void places left by the departing spirits. I loosen right thinking and perfect peace.

I ask for a hedge of fire around my mind and emotions. I now know that the Holy Spirit is in complete control of my mind. I prophetically decree that I have a spirit of power, of love, and a sound mind. Amen.

Peace

Lord this is your word and your word is truth:

John 16:33 TLB *I have told you all this so that you may have peace in me. Here on earth you will have many trials and sorrows. But take heart, because I have overcome the world.*

Luke 2:14 NIV *Glory to God in the highest, and on earth peace to men on whom his favor rests.*

Luke 1:79 TLB *...to give light to those who sit in darkness and in the shadow of death, and to guide us to the path of peace.*

Galatians 5:22 NIV *But the fruit of the Spirit is: love, joy, peace, patience, kindness, goodness, faithfulness, gentleness, and self-control.*

2 Corinthians 13:11 TLB *Dear brothers and sisters, I close my letter with these last words: Rejoice. Change your ways. Encourage each other. Live in harmony and peace. Then the God of love and peace will be with you.*

Romans 8:6 TLB   *If your sinful nature controls your mind, there is death. But if the Holy Spirit controls your mind, there is life and peace.*

Romans 2:10 NIV   *But there will be glory, and honor, and peace for everyone who does good.*

Targeted Prayer:

Heavenly Father,

In the name of Jesus, I bind, break the soul-ties, break your power, and cast out of me the strongmen of lying spirits and fear as well as tormenting and harassing spirits. I demand you to separate from me now. Go to the arid places never to return. You cannot attach yourself to anyone or anything.

Holy Spirit cover me with your peace as the enemy has overwhelmed me with fear, doubt, and unbelief. I prophetically decree that the God of peace will soon crush Satan under my feet, and that the grace of our Lord Jesus Christ is with me. (Romans 16:20 NIV) I also decree that the Holy Spirit controls my mind where there is life and peace. And the peace you give isn't like the peace the world gives. I will not be troubled or afraid. (John 14:27 NIV) Amen.

Protection

Lord, this is your word and your word is truth:

2 Thessalonians 3:3 NIV   *But the Lord is faithful, and he will strengthen and protect you from the evil one.*

1 Peter 5:7 TLB   *Give all your worries and cares to God, for he cares about what happens to you.*

Luke 10:19 TLB   *And I have given you authority over all the power of the enemy, and you can walk among snakes and scorpions and crush them. Nothing will injure you.*

Proverbs 1:33 NIV   *... but whoever listens to me will live in safety and be at ease, without fear of harm.*

Psalms 7:10 TLB   *God is my shield; saving those whose hearts are true and right.*

Psalms 5:12 NIV   *For surely, O Lord, you bless the righteous; you surround them with your favor as with a shield.*

Psalms 57:2-3 NIV   *I cry out to God Most High, to God, who fulfills his purpose for me. He sends from heaven and saves me, rebuking those who hotly pursue me; God sends his love and his faithfulness.*

Psalms 34:7 TLB   *For the angel of the Lord guards all who fear him, and he rescues them.*

Psalms 145:20 TLB   *The Lord protects all those who love him, but he destroys the wicked.*

Psalms 121:7-8 TLB   *The Lord keeps you from all evil and preserves your life. The Lord keeps watch over you as you come and go, both now and forever.*

Psalms 138:7 TLB   *Though I am surrounded by troubles, you will preserve me against the anger of my enemies. You will clench your fist against my angry enemies! Your power will save me.*

Targeted Prayer:

Heavenly Father,

In the name of Jesus, I pray that you would protect me from bacterial or viral infections, diseases, or other infirmities that would try to kill, steel, or destroy my body. I ask for your right hand to save me from accidents, dangers, plans, and schemes of the enemy.

Be my fortress, strength, shield, and stronghold. Let me dwell and if necessary hide in the shadow of your wings. Be my rock, salvation, and defense so that I will not be moved or shaken.

Lord, I am asking for the gift of discernment, and wisdom that will preserve me from all evil.

I demand that all forms of evil communication are severed, and the demonic spirits are rendered deaf and dumb.

I decree that I will use mightily all the heavenly power and authority available to me to tread on serpents and scorpions and over all the power of the enemy.

I will stand firm and resist the devil. The enemy will flee at the sound of the Sword of the Spirit as it springs forth from my mouth. It will be as rushing waters filled with life and truth. There is no weapon formed against me that will succeed. Amen.

Trust

Lord this is your word and your word is truth:

1 John 4:16 TLB *We know how much God loves us, and we have put our trust in him. God is love, and all who live in love live in God, and God lives in them.*

1 Peter 4:19 TLB *So if you are suffering according to God's will, keep on doing what is right, and trust yourself to the God who made you, for he will never fail you.*

1 Peter 1:8 TLB *You love him even though you have never seen him. Though you do not see him, you trust him; and even now you are happy with a glorious, inexpressible joy.*

Hebrews 10:35 TLB *Do not throw away this confident trust in the Lord, no matter what happens. Remember the great reward it brings you!*

Ephesians 3:17 TLB *And I pray that Christ will be more and more at home in your hearts as you trust in him. May your roots go down deep into the soil of God's marvelous love.*

Proverbs 3:5 NIV *Trust in the Lord with all your heart and lean not on your own understanding; in all your ways acknowledge him, and he will make your paths straight.*

Targeted Prayer:

Heavenly Father,

In the name of Jesus, I bind, break the soul-ties, break your power, and cast out of me the strongmen of fear and lying spirits. I demand you to separate from me now. Go to the arid places, and never return. You cannot attach yourself to anyone or anything.

Lord, I ask you to increase my trust in you. May my roots go down deep into the rich soil of your marvelous love. I ask for a hedge of protection around my mind and thoughts.

I will no longer listen to the lying spirits. As the lies enter my thoughts, I will rebuke them immediately. There will only be positive words that flow from my mouth because *"...for out of the overflow of the heart the mouth speaks."* (Luke 6:45 NIV) I decree that my faith, trust, and hope are now placed confidently in you. Amen.

Joy

Lord this is your word and your word is truth:

Acts 2:26 NIV   *Therefore my heart is glad and my tongue rejoices; my body will live in hope.*

Psalms 30:11 NIV   *You turned my wailing into dancing. You removed my sackcloth and clothed me with joy.*

Psalms 31:7 TLB   *I am overcome with joy because of your unfailing love, for you have seen my troubles; and you care about the anguish of my soul.*

Targeted Prayer:

Holy Spirit, I ask for peace and joy to flow into the innermost parts of my body, and spring forth like rushing waters over my body, soul, and spirit. Your scriptures say, *"No wonder my heart is filled with joy, and my mouth shouts his praises! My body rests in safety."* (Psalms 16:9 TLB)

I prophetically decree that you have brought joy to my heart. Amen.

CHAPTER FOUR

Targeted Prayers for the victim and the family to pray for the abuser:

Salvation

Pride

Deliverance

Generational Curses

Bondage

Mental Strongholds

Holiness

Salvation

Lord, this is your word and your word is truth:

John 3:16 NIV   *For God so loved the world, that he gave his one and only Son, that whosoever believes in him shall not perish but have eternal life.*

Titus 2:11 NIV   *For the grace of God that brings salvation has appeared to all men.*

1 Peter 1:23 TLB   *For you have been born again. Your new life did not come from your earthly parents because the life they gave you will end in death. But this new life will last forever because it comes from the eternal, living Word of God.*

Romans 10:13 TLB   *For anyone who calls on the name of the Lord will be saved.*

John 3:3 TLB   *Jesus replied, "I assure you, unless you are born again, you can never see the kingdom of God."*

Targeted Prayer:

Heavenly Father,

I ask for your wisdom and revelation as we plant the seeds of salvation in _____'s mind.

In the name of Jesus, I bind the strongmen of error, lying spirits, bondage, anti-Christ, and spirit of rebellion over _____. Lord, I ask you to sever all forms of evil communication that is hindering _____'s salvation, and to render the demonic spirits deaf and dumb.

I prophetically decree that _____ will accept you as his/her Lord and Savior. For you said, *"For anyone who calls on the name of the Lord will be saved."* (Romans 10:13 TLB) I decree that you, God the Father, and the Holy Spirit will reign in _____ life.

I decree that there is a holy fire burning deep within _____. I decree that he/she will go directly into the plans you have for him/her. *"Many are the plans in a man's heart, but it is the Lord's purpose that prevails."* (Proverbs 19:21 NIV)

Lord Jesus, you were sent *"into the world not to condemn the world, but that the world through you might be saved."* (John 3:17 NIV) I decree that _____ is saved through you. Amen.

Pride

Lord, this is your word and your word is truth:

Proverbs 8:13 *To fear the Lord is to hate evil; I hate pride and arrogance, evil behavior and perverse speech.*

Proverbs 11:2 *When pride comes, then comes disgrace, but with humility comes wisdom.*

Proverbs 16:18 *Pride goes before destruction, a haughty spirit before a fall.*

Proverbs 29:23 *A man's pride brings him low, but a man of lowly spirit gains honor.*

Targeted Prayer:

Heavenly Father,

According to your word, *"Pride goes before destruction; a haughty spirit before a fall."* (Proverbs 16:18) Lord, _____ has not *"... denied himself/herself, picked up his/her cross daily, and followed you."* (Luke 9:23)

He/she has allowed the strongman of pride a foothold in his/her life. He/she believes the strongman of lying spirits, and the spirits of deception and confusion.

Because pride is so deceptive, I pray that you will take his/her mind captive; and you will show him/her every prideful seed that has taken root in his/her life.

I believe the leviathan spirit and spirit of jezebel may also have control over _____. In the name of Jesus, I bind the leviathan spirit, jezebel spirit, strongman of pride, spirit of rebellion, and stubbornness within_____. Lord, I ask you to expose and destroy the roots of the leviathan spirit and jezebel spirit within him/her. I loosen in him/her a humble spirit; and with humility, comes wisdom. Lord, I decree that he/she is cleansed and purified. Thank you for your grace and mercy, Lord. Amen.

Note: The leviathan spirit carries the very nature and works of the accuser of the brethren. The first way that this spirit will attack is with his tongue. This spirit attacks out of his mouth with lies, gossip, accusation, criticism, faultfinding, and slander. He wants to slander your character and bring reproach on your name. This spirit twists words from his mouth. His main objective is to cause discord and division. Bible references are: Job 4, Isaiah 27:1, and Psalm 74:14

Deliverance

Lord this is your word and your word is truth:

John 8:32 NIV *Then you will know the truth, and the truth will set you free.*

2 Corinthians 3:17 NIV *Now the Lord is the Spirit: and where the Spirit of the Lord is, there is freedom.*

John 8:36 TLB *If the Son sets you free, you will indeed be free.*

1 John 3:8 TLB *...But the Son of God came to destroy these works of the devil.*

Psalms 129:4 NIV *But the Lord is righteous; he has cut me from the cords of the wicked.*

Proverbs 11:21 NIV *...but those who are righteous will go free.*

Targeted Prayer:

Heavenly Father,

Satan is the father of lies, and he is keeping him/her in bondage. Lord, break the yokes or bondages that Satan has placed on his/her life. Break down all barriers that are preventing _____ from hearing the truth and seeing the truth.

Lord, expose the roots of his/her ungodly behaviors. Bring all unrighteous behaviors to the light. Convict him/her of his/her unrighteousness. Upon his/her repentance, Lord, please heal all his/her spiritual, physical, emotional, verbal, and sexual wounds. Take all the fragmented pieces of his/her soul and restore it.

Holy Spirit, I ask you to come into his/her life with a burning fire that consumes everything that is not of God. I ask Holy Spirit that you immediately fill all void places left by the evil departures. He/she will overcome the enemy by the blood of the Lamb and by the word of their testimony.

I decree that because the Lord is righteous he has cut _____ from the cords of the wicked. I decree that he/she will know the truth, and the truth will set him/her free. Amen.

Generational Curses

Through conception, weaknesses and behavioral tendencies are passed down to us as a result of inheriting the iniquities of our fathers. Thereby, the curses are passed on to each successive generation as they commit the same sins.

Abusive behavior is most likely the result of hurts and wounds in a person's childhood; more than likely, those wounds and hurts have not been healed. Therefore, we are going to pray the following prayer for truth and healing to come forth.

Targeted Prayer:

By the authority and power given to me by the holy name of our Lord, Jesus Christ, I bind the strongmen of: the spirit of divination, familiar spirit, spirit of jealousy, lying spirit, perverse spirit, spirit of haughtiness, spirit of heaviness, spirit of whoredoms, spirit of infirmity, dumb and deaf spirit, spirit of bondage, spirit of fear, seducing spirits, spirit of anti-Christ, spirit of error, and spirit of death and all other demonic spirits that are associated with any and all generational curses within_____.

I loosen insights, revelation, and right thinking. Truth and conviction will come forth. I decree _____ will realize that he/she has made wrong choices, and has, as a result, harmed others.

I decree that true repentance will come forth. I decree that God will then begin the process of healing the abuser. Amen.

Bondage

This spirit usually works very closely with the spirit of fear.

Romans 8:15 NIV   *You did not receive a spirit that makes you a slave again to fear, but you received the Spirit of Sonship. And by him we cry, "Abba Father."*

If we are going to rule and reign with Christ as the Bible tells us, we must depart from the worldly things that lead us into bondage. It is a once-and-for-all decision that we have to consciously make in our heart.

Some of the manifestations of this spirit are addiction to drugs, alcohol, cigarettes, food, gambling, and unnatural sex acts. On the other extreme of gluttony are anorexia nervosa and bulimia.

Targeted Prayer:

Heavenly Father,

I come to you realizing that only you can free _____from Satan's web. Thank you for your great love.

In the name of Jesus Christ of Nazareth, I bind the strongmen of bondage and fear along with the spirits of addictions, death, captivity to Satan, bondage to sin, servant of corruption, and compulsive sin within _____. According to Matthew 18:18 NIV, it states, *"...whatsoever ye shall bind on earth shall be bound in heaven."* Satan is "a spiritual spider." It tries to bind and paralyze _____ with his cords of habits and bondage.

I loose righteousness in his/her life according to Matthew 18:18 NIV that promises, *"...whatsoever ye shall loose on earth shall be loosed in heaven."* Help him/her to be free forever from these bondages and addictions. I decree that he/she will walk in perfect freedom.

Holy Spirit please come and fill the void places within him/her. Amen.

Mental Strongholds

Lord this is your word and your word is truth:

Romans 12:2 NIV *Do not conform any longer to the pattern of this world, but be transformed by the renewing of your mind. Then you will be able to test and approve what God's will is - his good, pleasing, and perfect will.*

2 Corinthians 10:4-5 NIV *The weapons we fight with are not the weapons of the world. On the contrary, they have divine power to demolish strongholds. We demolish arguments and every pretension that sets itself up against the knowledge of God, and we take captive every thought to make it obedient to Christ.*

Romans 8:6 NIV *The mind of the sinful man is death, but the mind controlled by the Spirit is life and peace.*

Isaiah 26:3 NIV *You will keep in perfect peace him whose mind is steadfast, because he trusts in you.*

2 Timothy 1:7 NIV *For God did not give us a spirit of timidity, but a spirit of power, of love and self-discipline.*

Targeted Prayer:

Heavenly Father,

He/she is having trouble keeping his/her mind in perfect peace. The enemy is creating mine fields in his/her mind, and as a result confusion reigns. If there are strongholds in his/her life that need to be destroyed, guide and direct _____ so that he/she can shut these open doors. If there is a forgiveness problem, convict him/her.

In the name of Jesus, I bind the strongmen of dumb and deaf spirits, lying spirits, familiar spirits, fear, and heaviness, as well as the spirits of mental illness, insanity, suicide, crying, familial spirits, dormant spirits, and confusion within _____. I loosen right thinking and peace in his/her body, soul, and spirit. Holy Spirit please fill all void places left by the departing spirits.

I ask for a hedge of fire around his/her mind and emotions. I decree that he/she will walk in perfect peace knowing that the Holy Spirit is in complete control of his/her mind. I prophetically decree that he/she has a spirit of power, of love, and a sound mind. Amen.

Holiness

Lord, this is your word and your word is truth:

Isaiah 35:8 NIV *And a highway will be there; it will be called the Way of Holiness. The unclean will not journey on it; it will be for those who walk in that Way; wicked fools will not go about on it*

Isaiah 29:23 NIV *When they see among them their children, the work of my hands, they will keep my name holy; they will acknowledge the holiness of the Holy One of Jacob, and will stand in awe of the God of Israel.*

Ezekiel 38:23 NIV *And so I will show my greatness and my holiness, and I will make myself known in the sight of many nations. Then they will know that I am the Lord.*

Romans 6:22 NIV *But now that you have been set free from sin and have become slaves to God, the benefit you reap leads to holiness, and the result is eternal life.*

1 Corinthians 1:30 NIV   *It is because of him that you are in Christ Jesus, who has become for us wisdom from God - that is, our righteousness, holiness, and redemption.*

2 Corinthians 7:1 NIV   *Since we have these promises, dear friends, let us purify ourselves from everything that contaminates body and spirit, perfecting holiness out of reverence for God.*

Romans 6:19 NIV   *Put this in human terms because you are weak in your natural selves. Just as you used to offer the parts of your body in slavery to impurity and to ever-increasing wickedness, so now offer them in slavery to righteousness leading to holiness.*

Ephesians 4:24 NIV   *...and to put on the new self, created to be like God in true righteousness and holiness.*

Hebrews 12:14 NIV   *Make every effort to live in peace with all men and to be holy; without holiness no one will see the Lord.*

1 Chronicles 16:29 NIV   *Ascribe to the Lord the glory due his name. Bring an offering and come before him; worship the Lord in the splendor of his holiness.*

Targeted Prayer:

Heavenly Father,

I decree that he/she will be convicted of all sin. I decree that you, Lord, will bring deliverance to all his/her unrighteousness.

I decree that he/she will purify his/her self from everything that contaminates his/her body, soul, and spirit, perfecting holiness out of reverence for you. I decree that he/she will put on the new self, created to be like God in true righteousness and holiness.

I decree that he/she will live in peace with all men and be holy. I decree that he/she is in your hands. I decree that he/she will walk on the highway of holiness. Amen.

Books and References

Abuse
1. stoprelationabuse.org
2. Psychologicalabuse – Wikipedia
3. National Intimate Partner and Sexual violence Survey 2010
4. Bureau of Justice Statistics Crime Data
5. Frieze I.H. Brown: ***Violence in Marriage***
6. M.H. Tonry: Univ. of Chicago Press, ***Family Violence***
7. Escapeabuse.com
8. Embracing Justice: ***A Resource guide for Rabbis on Domestic Violence.***
9. womenslaw.org
10. ncadv.org, National Coalition Against Domestic Violence
11. Helene L. Taylor.org, preparations

Codependent Behavior
1. recoveryconnection.com
2. interventiontreatmentrecovery.org

Cover
1. Judy H Farris-Smith, 123.rf.com

Generational /Curses
1. ***Merriam-Webster's Collegiate Dictionary*** 1994, 1995
2. Rebecca Brown, M.D., ***Unbroken Curses***, (New Kensington, PA: Whitaker House, 1995)

Leviathan Spirit
1. thelordmybanner.com
2. demonbusters.com

Prayers
1. Judy H Farris-Smith, ***Targeted Prayers***, (Copyright @ 2011, 2017 by Little Sparrow Ministries, Lindale, Texas)

Setting Your Boundaries
1. Anne Katherine MA, *Where You End and I Begin*, (Copyright @ 1991 Parkside Publishing Corporation, Park Ridge, Illinois 60068)
2. www.make-my-life-work.com
Jesus Set Boundaries
3. www.soulshepherding.org
4. I Am Global Church

Soul-Ties
1. Bill and Sue Banks, *Breaking Unhealthy Soul-Ties,* (Kirkwood, MO: Impact Christian Books, Inc. 1999, 2001)

Spirit of Rejection
1. Chris Hayward, *The End of Rejection,* (Ventura, CA: Copyright @ 2007 by Regal Books)
2. Sermoncentral.com
3. Judy H Farris-Smith, *Setting Yourself Free, Deliverance from Darkness,* Copyright @ 2013, 2017 by Little Sparrow Ministries, Lindale, Texas)

Spoken Word
1. Charles Capps, *The Tongue – A Creative Force*, (Tulsa, OK: Harrison House, Inc., 1995, 1976)
2. Francis Frangipane, *Three Battlegrounds* (Cedar Rapids, IA: Advancing Church Publications, 1989)

Strongmen
1. Dr. Carol Robeson, *Strongman's His Name…What's His Game?* (Keizer, OR: Shiloh Publishing House, 1983, 1996)

Your Spiritual Authority
1. Kenneth Hagin, ***The Believer's Authority***, (Copyright ©1986 RHEMA Bible Church AKA Kenneth Hagin Ministries, Inc., Tulsa, OK 74150-0126)

Word Curses/Judgments/Spoken Word
1. Charles Capps**, *The Tongue – A Creative Force,*** (Tulsa, OK: Harrison House, Inc 1995)
2. Francis Frangipane, ***Three Battlegrounds*** (Cedar Rapids, IA: Advancing Church Publications, 1989)
3. ***The World Book Dictionary*** 1981 Edition (Copyright @ 1981 by Doubleday & Company, Inc.)
4. Judy H Farris-Smith, ***Targeted Prayers***, (Copyright @ 2011, 2017 by Little Sparrow Ministries, Lindale, Texas)\

Other Books By Little Sparrow Ministries
Can be ordered on littlesparrowministries.com

Setting Yourself Free, Deliverance from Darkness (Little Sparrow Ministries, Copyright © 2013, 2017 Lindale, Texas 75771)

Targeted Prayers (Little Sparrow Ministries, Copyright © 2011, 2017, Lindale, Texas 75771)

Set Yourself Free Little Children and Come to Me (Little Sparrow Ministries, Copyright © 2003, 2017 Lindale, Texas 75771)

Truth vs. Lies, Information for Teenagers (Little Sparrow Ministries, Copyright © 2008, 2017 Lindale, Texas 75771)

Little Bit, the Miracle Kid (Little Sparrow Ministries, Copyright © 2009 Lindale, Texas 75771)

Have Faith, Inspirational Testimonies (Little Sparrow Ministries, Copyright © 2011 Lindale, Texas 75771)

Collection of Letters from the Father's Heart (Little Sparrow Ministries, Copyright © 2017 Lindale, Texas 75771)

Freedom (Little Sparrow Ministries, Copyright © 2017 Lindale, Texas 75771)

Intersession for the Men in Your Life (Little Sparrow Ministries, Copyright © 2017 Lindale, Texas 75771)

He is in the Middle of Your Fire, Spiritual Workbook for PTSD (Little Sparrow Ministries, Copyright © 2017 Lindale, Texas 75771)

www.ingramcontent.com/pod-product-compliance
Lightning Source LLC
LaVergne TN
LVHW011730060526
838200LV00051B/3104